# TRAILBLAZERS OF THE WILD WEST

# PIONEERING WOMEN
## OF THE WILD WEST

Jeff Savage

ENSLOW PUBLISHERS, INC.

44 Fadem Road
Box 699
Springfield, N.J. 07081
U.S.A.

P.O. Box 38
Aldershot
Hants GU12 6BP
U.K.

Copyright © 1995 by Jeff Savage.

**Library of Congress Cataloging-in-Publication Data**

Savage, Jeff, 1961–
    Pioneering women of the Wild West / Jeff Savage.
       p. cm. — (Trailblazers of the Wild West)
    Includes bibliographical references and index.
    ISBN 0-89490-604-6
    1. Women pioneers—West (U.S.)—History—19th century—Juvenile literature.
2. Women—West (U.S.)—History—19th century—Juvenile literature. 3. West
(U.S.)—Social life and customs—Juvenile literature. [1. Pioneers. 2. Women—West
(U.S.) 3. West (U.S.)—Social life and customs.] I. Title. II. Series.
F596.S236 1995
978′.02—dc20                                                                94-32324
                                                                                    CIP
                                                                                     AC

Printed in the United States of America

10 9 8 7 6 5 4 3 2 1

**Illustration Credits:** Arizona Historical Society Library, p. 36; Denver
Public Library, Western History Department, pp. 13, 20, 30, 33, 38; Diction-
ary of American Portraits (Dover Publications, Inc., 1967), p. 40 (left);
Kansas State Historical Society, p. 42; Library of Congress, pp. 11, 23, 27;
Kristin McCarthy, pp. 16, 28; Montana Historical Society, p. 21; Courtesy
Tamiment Institute, p. 40 (right); Western History Collections, University
of Oklahoma Library, pp. 25, 35; Wyoming State Museum, pp. 4, 8, 18.

**Cover Illustration:** Paul Daly

# ⋙❂ CONTENTS ❂⋘

*Western women were not afraid to use guns.*

# ⚔ 1 ⚔

# DEFENDING THE HOME

———————◆•◆•◆———————

Agnes Morley stared out the window. She watched the
sheriff's deputy and some other men in the corral. They
were rounding up several cattle to be taken away. Agnes
was angry with the men for taking her cattle. But there
was nothing she could do to stop it.

Agnes lived with her mother, sister, and brother.
When her father died a few years earlier, in 1886, the rest
of the Morleys moved to a ranch in New Mexico, high
in the Datil Mountains. They became cattle ranchers.

Agnes learned the ways of ranching before she was
a teenager. She learned about different breeds of cattle,
and she worked at herding. She even learned to beat
rustlers, or cattle thieves, at their own game. When the
rustlers stole some cattle, she and her brother would
follow them, wait for a chance, and steal them right

back. Because of her life on the ranch, Agnes became an expert horse rider.

On this day, the Morley family owed money. It was common for ranchers to be in debt sometimes. Instead of letting them pay what they owed when they sold some cattle, the sheriff demanded payment right away. He declared that the Morleys would have to give up some of their cattle to sell at auction. The sheriff sent his deputy and some cowhands over to the family ranch to seize the cattle. The sheriff promised to leave the Morleys' horses alone. They would take only cattle.

Agnes watched as the deputy finished up in the corral. She never had cared much for the deputy. She thought he was dishonest, and cruel to animals.

Suddenly, the deputy ran into the barn. In the next moment he reappeared with her horse. He led it by the reins out to the main road where the cowhands were waiting with the cattle. The deputy was taking away her horse. The way Agnes figured it, he was stealing it!

Agnes wasn't about to let the deputy steal her horse. She raced to the barn, mounted another horse, and galloped off after him.

Agnes spotted the deputy standing on the road with several cowboys. Then she saw her horse. Agnes rode up to the deputy and demanded her horse back. The deputy refused. Agnes went after her horse anyway. She jumped to the ground in a somersault, then ran over to her horse. When the deputy tried to stop her, Agnes picked up a strap with a heavy bell on the end. She warned the deputy not to interfere. "One step closer," she yelled, "and I'll brain you with this bell!"[1] The deputy backed away. Agnes rode off on her own horse, leading the other one. The cowboys who were with the deputy later told Agnes that they had been ready to come to her defense. They even said they would have used their guns. As it turned out, Agnes didn't need any help.

Most women were highly appreciated in the early days of the West. This is partly because there were not many of them. In 1849, for example, fewer than five thousand women were among the fifty thousand people who traveled west. Women were precious because they were scarce.

Even ruthless gunslingers were kind to most pioneer women. Agnes experienced this one night when she was out riding alone. An outlaw on the run, in need of a good horse, approached her on the trail. "Good evening, Miss," he said politely as he passed her.[2] A short time later, the sheriff caught that outlaw in the act of stealing a horse from a corral, and killed him. The outlaw could have stolen Agnes's horse. He even could have killed her and then taken it. Instead, the outlaw respected her. It cost him his life.

Agnes began carrying a gun. She called it her "equalizer." It had been rare for women in the West to arm themselves, but they did not like to be viewed as

*Women had to help on the farm. They had to know how to ride a horse and how to use a hoe to aid their husbands. The harsh conditions of the West often made this necessary.*

helpless. Agnes later wrote a book about her life. In her book, she said, "A six-shooter does give one a sense of security. We had a saying, 'A six-shooter makes all men equal.' I amended it to, 'A six-shooter makes men and women equal.'"[3]

As she grew older, Agnes continued to help her mother run the cattle operation. She enjoyed her freedom to roam the range, and she felt sorry for the women who were confined by their husbands. Most women did not get the chance to be cattle ranchers. It was considered "man's work."

Agnes knew that this sort of treatment wasn't fair, so she rebelled. First, she refused to wear a sunbonnet.

8

Instead, she wore a five-gallon Stetson cowboy hat. Men were surprised at her boldness, and many respected her even more. Next, she wore a blue flannel shirt and blue denim pants. She completed her outfit with fancy cowboy boots. Finally, instead of riding sidesaddle, as was the custom for women, Agnes began riding her horse astride with her feet in the stirrups.

Agnes Morley was admired by many who knew her. She was strong, outspoken, and confident. In a way, she blazed her own trail on the frontier. As a woman who made a difference, however, she was not alone in the West.

Many hardships were faced as people settled the western United States in the mid- to late 1800s. The vast wilderness teemed with unknown dangers. There was always a threat of death by thirst, hunger, freezing, animal attack, and a dozen other terrors. Native Americans who tried to protect their land against the settlers posed another danger.

Many women came in from the East with their families to meet the challenges of the West. Other women traveled west to make their own way. These women found opportunities as enormous as the land itself. They traveled by covered wagon, by horse, and on foot. They rounded up or rustled cattle, robbed banks, panned for gold, taught school, hunted for food, died in gun battles, and demanded law and order. And they endured as best they could.

# ⟫⟪ 2 ⟫⟪

# THE FIRST WESTERN WOMEN

In 1876, a Native American woman named Bright Eyes La Flesche wrote for her father, the chief of the tribe: "Look ahead and you will see nothing but the white man, the future is full of the white man, and we shall be as nothing before him."[1]

For thousands of years, people have lived west of the Mississippi River in what is now the western United States. Scientists believe that the Native Americans originated in northern Asia. They probably first crossed over the Bering Strait from Siberia to Alaska around 12,000 years ago. It is believed that at that time a land bridge there connected Asia and North America.

As these peoples grew in number and spread out all across North and South America, many different cultures developed. Native Americans from the western

United States are very different from those in the
Amazon region of South America. Even in the West
there was great diversity. The roles of women in these
societies varied widely.

In general, the roles of Native American women
were not much different from those of American women
living in the East. Most of their lives revolved around
home and family. Marriage was very important and was
sometimes arranged by families. As adults, Native
American women were responsible for finding,
planting, and preparing food. They set up their

*Two Blackfoot women at home in their tipi.*

homes—lodges, tipis, wickiups, or pueblos. They raised their children, and taught them the ways of their people.

However, there were some differences. Native American women had some freedoms that white American women did not have. Sometimes women took part in council meetings. It was also usually easier to divorce among Native Americans than in American society. At the same time, some groups also treated women as slaves. Others practiced polygamy: a man could have more than one wife.

## Wives for Sale

Some of the first white people to visit the West were fur trappers and traders. Native Americans usually welcomed these strangers, regarding them as friends. Some of these pioneers and trappers married Native American women. Others bought women from those groups that treated women as slaves. A price of two horses or several pounds of beads or furs would be paid to a tribe in exchange. A Native American wife was especially useful to a trapper. She knew the land, and how and where to find food. She also knew how to prepare medicines from wild plants.

## Sacajawea

The first woman of the West to gain fame was Sacajawea. She was born a Shoshoni in what is today the state of Idaho. When she was about ten, Sacajawea was kidnapped by a Mandan war party. She was taken as a

*Sacajawea led Meriwether Lewis and William Clark on their journey to the Pacific coast.*

slave to what is today North Dakota. Several years later, Toussaint Charbonneau, a French Canadian fur trapper, purchased Sacajawea from the Mandan.

In 1804, when Sacajawea was about fifteen, a group of white men arrived at the village where she and Charbonneau lived. Meriwether Lewis and William Clark were on a journey across the continent. They were trying to reach the Pacific Ocean. The journey meant crossing the massive Rocky Mountains and traveling through a land inhabited by many Native American peoples.

Toussaint Charbonneau knew sign language. He joined the Lewis and Clark expedition as an interpreter. The exploration party, which consisted of thirty-two men and one woman—Sacajawea—was called the Corps of Discovery.

As the group waited for the last snow to thaw, Sacajawea gave birth to a boy. She named him Pomp.

When the group set off, Sacajawea carried Pomp on her back.

The group traveled through prairies filled with flowers and geese, and plains teeming with buffalo, elk, antelope, and deer. There were plenty of menacing grizzly bears and rattlesnakes, too. Lewis and Clark quickly realized that Sacajawea was expert at finding roots and berries.

The mere presence of Sacajawea and her baby saved the Lewis and Clark expedition from attack countless times. Native Americans knew that a war party would not bring along a woman and a baby.

One day, Sacajawea proved to be heroic. The group was traveling up the Missouri River. Most of the men were stumbling along the shore, using rope to pull the boats against a strong current. Others stayed in the boats as they were pulled along. Sacajawea was in the back of the boat that carried important equipment and documents. The boat tipped to one side. Water poured in. Several men panicked and fell overboard. Sacajawea remained calm. She scooped up all the valuable charts and maps that had fallen overboard. She then helped bail the water from the boat, keeping it afloat. Everyone was amazed at Sacajawea's bravery. A few days later, Lewis and Clark named a river after her.

On November 8, 1805, the Corps of Discovery reached the Pacific Ocean. The courageous Native American woman is still remembered to this day. In fact, there are more memorials of Sacajawea across the West than any other woman in American history. The most famous memorial of Sacajawea is a statue unveiled in 1905 in Portland, Oregon. The statue shows Sacajawea, proudly pointing the way, carrying Pomp on her back.

## Spanish America

Native Americans were not alone in the West before American settlers came. Much of what is now the far western and southwestern United States once was part of Mexico. From the 1500s until 1821 this region and what is now Mexico were part of Spain's American colonies. The Spanish developed a large colonial empire that stretched from the tip of South America to northern California.

The Spanish tried to set up settlements in what is now the United States. They were not very successful. There were a few sparse settlements centered mostly around missions that had been founded by Franciscan monks. The city of Santa Fe, in what is now New Mexico, was the only large settlement in the region. Spanish women probably first permanently settled as the wives of Spanish soldiers.

When white settlers began to move into Texas and California in the 1830s, it is guessed that there were several thousand Mexicans living there. In 1836, the people of Texas revolted against Mexico and declared their independence. In 1845, the United States annexed

Texas, setting off the Mexican War. After two years of fighting, American soldiers marched into Mexico City. Mexico gave up the southwest (today's Texas, New Mexico, Arizona, California, Nevada, Utah, and part of Colorado) to the victorious United States. In return, the United States paid Mexico $15 million for the territory. Soon, the Native American and Mexican societies would be overwhelmed by a flood of white settlers with little respect for other cultures.

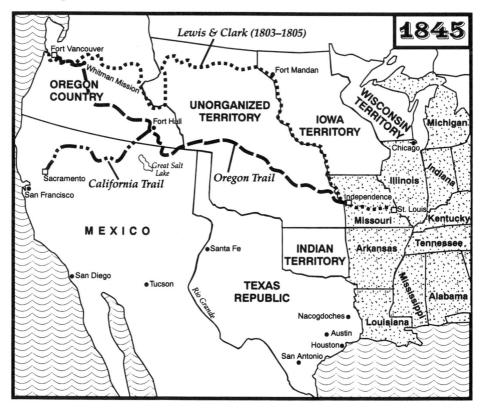

*When American pioneers blazed the California and Oregon Trails in the 1840s, California was still part of Mexico, and the Oregon Country was up for grabs between the United States and Great Britain.*

# ✦❁ 3 ❁✦

# HARD LIVING

---

Sarah Sim and her husband, Francis, left their New England home with their three children in 1856 to buy 160 acres on the plains of what today is Nebraska. They lived in a tiny log cabin and owned three cows, two oxen, several pigs and hens, and a horse. They hunted rabbits and chickens and gathered wild strawberries and plums. When a severe winter came, one of the Sim's children died of whooping cough. Francis became ill and was bedridden. Sarah's hand got infected. One of her fingers had to be cut off.

Feeling ill and lonely, Sarah fell into despair. For nearly a year, she appeared insane. She bit herself and her children. She shredded her clothes, destroyed her possessions, and even attempted suicide.

Somehow Sarah Sim began to recover. Francis's

illness subsided enough for him to plant crops. He grew potatoes and corn. Other settlers arrived and soon a school was built. Sarah planted a flower garden. She gave birth to another child; eventually, she gave birth to nine children. Five of them died young in the harsh conditions of the plains. Sarah remained strong as she lived the rest of her days in the rugged West.

## East Meets West

By the mid-nineteenth century women's roles had changed little since white settlers first set foot in North America more than three hundred years before. The

*Life on the plains was lonely for many pioneer women. Often there were no neighbors for miles and miles.*

typical pioneering woman in the West maintained the traditional role of housekeeper for her family. This meant cooking, sewing, washing clothes, milking cows, keeping a clean house and looking after the children. For most women in the West, it also meant doing heavy farm work and learning to shoot a gun, to hunt for food or to protect the home against strangers. Women could not afford to be passive or dependent in the rugged circumstances of their lives in the West.

For those city women who had not been poor back East, the rigors of pioneer life were especially difficult. Things that they had taken for granted before became impossible in the West. Keeping a clean house was almost impossible in a log cabin with a dirt floor. Farm women found the change less difficult, although there were problems that even they were not prepared for.

The West was clearly a different place than the East. It was a vast region with very few people in it. Neighbors were often many miles away. Life on the frontier often was isolated and lonely. The climate was hot and dry in the summer, and cold in the winter. There were few trees on the flat prairies and in the rugged mountain ranges. Death seemed to shadow the settlers.

At that time, there was often no treatment for what seem like harmless diseases today. Many times, there were no doctors for hundreds of miles. There were also no other women nearby to help a woman giving birth. As a result, many women died in childbirth. Children

*Living on the frontier involved a lot of hard work.*

often did not live past the first few months of life; many more did not reach the age of ten.

## Narcissa Whitman

Word of the Lewis and Clark expedition eventually spread to the cities in the East. The frontier West now seemed a safer place to explore. For the next thirty years, trappers scoured the mountains and forests of the region for beaver pelts. The land was open and free.

In 1836, a gathering of mountain men at the Green River were met with an astonishing sight: two white women! They were part of a group traveling to Oregon territory that had reached what today is Wyoming. Narcissa Whitman and Eliza Spalding were believed by many to be the first white women to cross the Rocky Mountains. The purpose of the group was to establish a mission at Fort Walla Walla, in what is now the state of Washington. They hoped to bring their religion to the white settlers and Native Americans of the West.

The journey to Oregon territory was grueling. When Whitman finally reached her destination, she described the trek as "an unheard of journey for females."[1] At this point, the traveling party chose to split apart. Whitman and her husband, Marcus, decided to live among the Cayuse people. It was primitive living, but she and Marcus made the best of it. They built a house and a barn. Crops were planted and harvested. They taught

*Churches were often distant from isolated farms. When they were near, they provided the settlers with a sense of community.*

the Cayuse new ways to grow food. In the spring, Whitman gave birth to a baby girl and named her Alice.

More and more people continued to journey westward on what had become known as the Oregon Trail. When wagon trains on the trail arrived at Whitman's home, she greeted the weary travelers with food. Then tragedy struck. Little Alice wandered away from the house one day to the Walla Walla River. She fell in and drowned. Whitman was overwhelmed with grief. She held her dead baby in her arms for four days before allowing her to be buried. Whitman's home would forever be recognized as the one with the tombstone and little white picket fence in front of it.

## The Overland Trail

Many brave women trudged over rugged mountains and across arid plains to reach a new life in the West. Nancy Kelsey was among the first group of overland emigrants who reached California in 1841. These emigrants abandoned their covered wagons in order to cross the Sierra Nevada Mountains. They walked the last five hundred miles to the Pacific coast. Kelsey carried a young child with her the entire way.

Three years later, another group became the first emigrants to cross the Sierras in wagons. Among the group was Mary Bulgar Murphy, who made the grueling trip while pregnant. She gave birth the day after the group had cleared the last mountain range.

In 1849, some pioneers attempted to cross Death Valley and the Mojave Desert in California. They had to walk for miles at a time without water, and many died along the way. One who survived was Juliet Brier, a small woman with two children. She sometimes had to carry one of her children on her back. Men often begged Brier to turn back. She would courageously respond, "Every step I take will be toward California."[2] When she reached her destination along with the other survivors, she was roundly praised.

*Chinese-American children pose in nineteenth century Denver, Colorado. In the mid-1800s, many Chinese men came to the United States to earn money mining for gold or building railroads. Few brought their wives and children. Most planned to eventually return to China.*

# ❈ 4 ❈

# INDEPENDENCE

———◆—●—●—◆———

Independent women often were attracted to the freedom of the West. There, without the pressures of society, they could live pretty much as they pleased. As they learned to cope with harsh living conditions, their independence was reinforced. They were determined to have a voice in important matters. Many women began to challenge the authority of men.

## Speaking Up

Sam Houston, a distinguished general in the Texas-Mexican War, was confronted one day in 1836 by a woman named Pamela Mann. The general had borrowed some oxen from Mann's ranch to pull cannons over the muddy trail to Nacogdoches, telling her that the oxen would be used only to get to Nacogdoches. When General Houston ordered the army toward Harrisburg, Mann rode off to reclaim her oxen. After riding ten miles, she caught up with the army and demanded the return of her oxen. "General, you told me a damn lie," she said. "You said that you was going on the Nacogdoches road. Sir, I want my oxen." When General Houston explained that the cannons could not be moved without the oxen, she roared, "I don't care a damn for your cannon. I want my oxen."[1] The woman pulled out her gun on the general. She jumped off her horse, cut the oxen loose, remounted, and rode off with her animals.

*Women cowhands became regular features of many Wild West shows. These young women worked for the 101 Ranch in Oklahoma.*

## Calamity Jane

Another independent woman was Martha Jane Canary, also known as Calamity Jane. She had a reputation as a woman who did as she pleased. Calamity Jane liked to drink liquor straight from the bottle, smoke cigars, gamble, and tell stories. She bragged that she had been an Army scout. Whether or not this was true, Calamity Jane did engage in a number of "unladylike" activities. She liked to ride up and down the streets of Rapid City, South Dakota, aboard a big red bull. Other women despised Calamity Jane. While working as a bartender, she was confronted in the saloon one day by a group of angry women who had scissors to cut off her hair. "I jumped off the bar into their midst," Calamity Jane said, "and before they could say 'sickem' I had them bowling."[2] Calamity Jane was friends with Wild Bill Hickok, and claimed to be married to him for a time. When she died in 1903, she was buried next to Wild Bill.

## Gamblers

The grit of such women inspired dozens of dime novels about heroines. Dime novels were inexpensive fiction adventure stories printed in paperback. The women in these novels faced terrifying odds, but were able to ride, rope, and shoot their way out of trouble. These stories were outrageous. But there were plenty of real-life women who encountered their share of adventure in the West.

*Martha Jane "Calamity Jane" Canary stands before the grave of Wild Bill Hickok. Though Hickok denied it, she claimed to be his wife. On her death, Calamity Jane was buried beside him.*

While her husband worked as a miner in Colorado, Alice Tuckert Tubbs frequented the gambling halls in the area. She studied the faces of the other poker players and learned to tell whether they were holding a good hand. She kept her own face expressionless while she played, prompting card players to dub her "Poker Alice." She won at poker almost every time and soon had enough money to open her own gambling houses in towns throughout the region.

Opening gaming halls was a risky business. During the gold rush days Eleanore Dumont convinced the miners of Nevada City, Nevada, that it was a privilege to lose their money at her gaming tables. She offered free champagne to all customers. After making a small fortune in Nevada, she then moved to Bodie, California, where she opened another gambling house. She did well at first, but one night she came up against an unusually lucky man and lost all her money. Distraught at going bankrupt all at once, Dumont walked out along the road, took a vial from her purse, and swallowed poison.

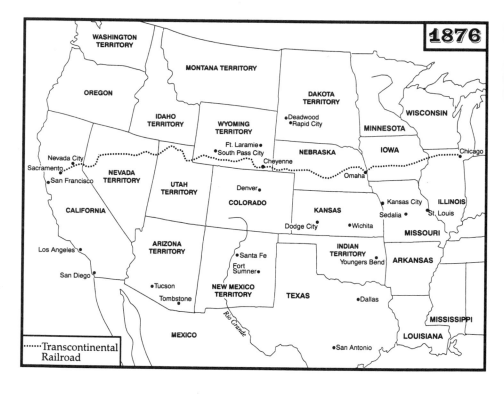

*By the 1870s the lines of the United States looked much as they do today. Most of the territories, however, were still largely empty of white settlers. It was during this time that the United States Army was at war with the Native American peoples.*

## Working the Mines

The gold rush of the mid-1800s was a wild frenzy as thousands of prospectors flooded remote areas. Boom towns sprang up, and with them came opportunities. Many women opened supply shops. Others worked as cooks, barmaids and dancers. Some gritty women even tried their hand at mining.

Mining was a grueling business and it took endurance and patience to make a living at it. Louise Clappe was a successful miner in the rugged Sierra Nevada Mountains of California. She was known in the West as Dame Shirley. She wrote to her sister back in New England that she could never return to the East. "I like the wild and barbarous life," Dame Shirley said.[3]

## Nellie Cashman

Perhaps no other woman better embodied the courageous, independent woman of the West than miner Nellie Cashman. She traveled across the West, searching for gold from Alaska to Mexico. And she found plenty, too. She had such nicknames as Frontier Angel, the Miner's Angel, the Angel of Tombstone, and the Saint of the Sourdoughs. She was known for hitting pay dirt and for helping people. In her fifty years of prospecting, she struck it rich at least half a dozen times. Yet, she never kept any of her money. Nellie Cashman gave away everything she earned to people less fortunate than herself and who were unable to take care of themselves.

*Known as the Miner's Angel, Nellie Cashman became famous for her luck at finding gold. Rather than spend all her money on herself, she gave much of it away.*

She became one of the most famous western women of her day. One person simply called her "the best woman I ever knew."[4]

## Clara Brown

Clara Brown was born a slave. When she was freed, she went right to work washing men's shirts for 50 cents apiece. She invested her earnings in land, and within a few years, she managed to save $10,000. She did not spend her money frivolously. Instead, she used the money to help other ex-slaves get settled in Colorado. Clara Brown's courage, strength, and fortitude represented the true spirit of the women of the West.

# ⇥◀ 5 ▶⇤

# OUTLAWS

---

The independence and freedom of the West also bred another individual, the outlaw. While the vast majority of outlaws in the West were men, some women actively joined the ranks of thieves, gamblers, and outlaws.

## The Bandit Queen

Among the outlaws was Myra Belle Shirley, better known as Belle Starr. Sam Starr, her Cherokee husband, was an outlaw when Belle married him. Joining Sam in illegal activity, Belle became a famous horse thief, known throughout the West as the "Bandit Queen."

Belle was arrested several times for stealing horses. But it was difficult to convict her. She committed her crimes disguised as a man. Witnesses could not say for sure that the woman behind the disguise was Belle. She was convicted of horse theft only one time, and had to serve nine months in jail.

When Belle wasn't wearing a disguise, she was walking the streets with a pair of pearl-handled pistols at her sides. Sometimes she would shoot bullets into the air for fun.

Belle and Sam lived along the Canadian River at a place they named Younger's Bend. Before Belle married Sam, she was friends with Cole Younger, a notorious member of the James Gang. Younger's Bend became a popular hideout for outlaws. Belle told a local newspaper, "There are three or four jolly good fellows on the dodge now in my section, and when they come to my home they are welcome."[1]

## Cattle Kate

Belle was not the only famous woman thief. Ella Watson became known as Cattle Kate because she reportedly stole hundreds of cattle in Wyoming. Kate was twenty-six when she received 160 acres of land from the government. The Homestead Act of 1862 gave settlers public land to encourage them to inhabit land in the West. The Homestead Act did not please everyone. Ranchers grazing their cattle on the land were told to leave. It got harder for them to find grass for their cattle. Many ranchers fought back. This battle between the ranchers and the new settlers in Wyoming became known as the Johnson County War. Kate just happened to get caught in the middle of it.

Some people, including Kate's neighbor Jim Averill,

*Ella "Cattle Kate" Watson was accused of rustling cattle. Without benefit of a trial, Kate and her friend Jim Averill were hanged by an angry mob.*

said that Kate did not steal cattle. Many more claimed that Kate and Jim were responsible for the disappearance of many cows. True or not, they were killed for stealing.

On the sunny day of July 20, 1889, several armed men rode up on horses to Cattle Kate's cabin. She was ordered to climb aboard a wagon. When she hesitated, one of the men shouted, "Get into that wagon, or we'll rope and drag you."[2] The mob drove her to Jim's place, where they forced him into the wagon at gunpoint. The cattlemen then rode four miles to Spring Canyon, next to the Sweetwater River.

Cattle Kate and Jim Averill believed they were safe. But it wasn't so. The men made Cattle Kate and Jim stand on a rock under a tree. They threw lariats over a branch, tied nooses at the ends, and slipped them around the necks of Cattle Kate and Jim. Then they told the pair that they would be freed if they left the country. They refused. The cattlemen shoved them off the rock, and they both were hanged.

## Flora Quick

Other women involved in crime met an early death. Flora Quick was born to a wealthy family, but she was charmed by the lure of the West and so headed that way when she was a teenager. Quick earned a living trading for horses or money, then quit trading and began stealing. She disguised herself as a man, Tom King, during holdups. She joined the notorious Dalton Gang and charmed railroaders into giving her information about trains for the gang to rob. Quick later moved to Tombstone, Arizona, where "Tom King" was killed during an attempted holdup.

## Young Rustlers

Annie McDoulet and Jennie Stevens were two teenage outlaws who called themselves Cattle Annie and Little Britches. Cattle Annie was seventeen, and Little Britches was sixteen, when they fell in love with two dashing young outlaws they met at a community dance. The girls were captured in 1894 while they were riding with an outlaw gang that stole horses and cattle. They were sent to prison. After their release two years later, Annie and Jennie became law-abiding citizens.

*Cattle Annie and Little Britches got mixed up with an outlaw gang. After they were caught and sent to prison, the two young women lived law-abiding lives.*

## Pearl Hart

Pearl Hart was working as a cook in an Arizona mining camp when a drunken miner named Joe Boot convinced her to join him in robbing a stagecoach. The duo made off with $431, but then they got lost during their escape. They were caught by a posse three days later. Boot was sentenced to thirty-five years in prison. Hart was sentenced to five years, but she was released for good behavior halfway through her term. Hart was arrested again three years later for her part in a train robbery. She wised up after that and moved quietly to Kansas City.

## Etta Place

Etta Place became a well-known outlaw when she teamed up with Butch Cassidy and the Sundance Kid.

Etta and Harry Longabaugh, the Sundance Kid, met and fell in love at a dance hall. Place is believed by many to have planned some of the robberies for the gang, which was known as the Wild Bunch, and the Hole-in-the-Wall Gang. Trains, banks, and stagecoaches were never safe with Etta's gang nearby. She devised plans to use dynamite, and even a skunk, to pull off robberies. The gang eventually fled to Argentina where, some say, Butch and Sundance were killed in a shoot-out with authorities. Etta Place had returned to the United States for a minor operation several weeks earlier. She was never heard from again.

*After giving up her life of crime, Pearl Hart began a quiet life in Kansas City.*

# ✶◀ 6 ▶✶

# CHANGE AND REFORM

———◆━◆◆━◆———

One occupation readily available to many women was that of a schoolteacher. Americans stressed the importance of education for all. Some men, and almost all women, recognized the importance of an education despite the physical demands of the frontier. In many cases, a new settlement was barely opened before a schoolhouse was built. One group even organized a school district and paid taxes to build a school before any houses were built. When funds were not available, settlers turned their homes into makeshift schools to ensure the education of children.

## "The Duty of American Women"

Much of the credit for bringing education to the pioneers goes to Catharine Beecher. A well-educated New Englander who traveled in the Midwest in 1845, she discovered a serious lack of schooling for children. Catharine Beecher wrote a pamphlet called "The Duty of American Women to their Country," explaining the need for women to go West. In it, she wrote, "It is woman who is to come in at this emergency and meet the demand. . .woman, whom experience and testing have shown to be the best, as well as the cheapest, guardian and teacher of childhood."[1] Thousands of women responded to Beecher's cry for help. "Schoolmarms" soon became a source of pride and learning for the West.

*Schoolrooms on the frontier were often crude log cabins.*

## Suffrage

When independent women weren't busy tending to their farms, teaching, or panning for gold, they were taking charge of their lives in other ways, like fighting for women's rights.

September 6, 1870, was like any other day in the cities of the East. In a remote area in the West, however, it was a momentous day for women. The women of Wyoming formed lines in front of booths to cast their ballots in local elections.

The Nineteenth Amendment to the Constitution, giving women throughout the United States the right to vote in federal elections, would not be passed until 1920. But some states and territories in the West did not wait around for Congress to act. Women demanded the right to vote, and one state after another in the West gave in to this demand. In many cases, women campaigned mightily for years to earn this right.

Women won the vote in Wyoming fully half a century before the entire nation gained that right. This was accomplished through the efforts of a remarkable woman named Esther Hobart McQuigg Slack Morris. Morris was fifty-six years old when she moved to the mining boomtown of South Pass City, Wyoming. Women neighbors greeted her as they would any new citizen. They had no idea that she would win them the right to vote one year later.

Women in Kansas were fighting for the vote as well.

Susan B. Anthony made speeches in area churches. Lucy Stone traveled up to forty miles a day in a broken-down wagon to urge men to give in. Up north in South Dakota, Anna Howard Shaw pleaded with farmers across the frontier. None of these women pulled off as clever a trick like Esther Morris.

Morris gave a tea party and invited two prominent politicians who were running for the same seat in the Wyoming legislature. One was a Democrat. The other was a Republican. During the party, Morris managed to persuade the Democrat, William Bright, to promise that, if elected, he would introduce a bill to give women the right to vote. Morris was a good friend of the Democrat's

*Carrie Chapman Catt (left) and Anna Howard Shaw (right) were two pioneers in the women's suffrage movement. Shaw was president of the National American Women Suffrage Association from 1904 to 1915. Catt led the group from 1915 to 1947.*

wife, and even helped her during a troublesome child-birth. Hearing this promise, the Republican, H.G. Dick-erson, had no choice but to make the same promise. Morris had pulled off a perfect political stunt. William Bright won the election and lived up to his promise. He drafted a bill that was approved by enough fellow Demo-crats to present to the governor. It is believed that the Democrats were trying to embarrass the governor be-cause he was a rival Republican. If that was true, the plan backfired. Governor John A. Campbell quickly signed the bill to make it a law. From that day forward, women in Wyoming had the right to vote. Esther Morris had done it!

Other women, like Abigail Scott Duniway in Oregon and Carrie Chapman Catt in Idaho, won the right to vote for women in those states. Women also gained the right to run for public office. The state of Montana elected the first woman to Congress. Jeannette Rankin became a Congresswoman in 1917, three years before the Nine-teenth Amendment gave women throughout the United States the right to vote.

## Taking Action

Carry Nation, a Kansas widow, became a famous cru-sader against alcohol. Her first husband had died of alcoholism. Her method of fighting for her cause was to step into saloons and begin singing hymns loudly until bartenders got frustrated and physically threw her out.

*Carry Nation led the fight against alcohol in the West. She became famous for busting up saloons with a hatchet. Here she is under arrest for disturbing the peace.*

The bartenders would then be arrested for assault and their saloons would be shut down. Eventually, Carry Nation used a hatchet to chop up bars. She continued to wield her hatchet in saloons throughout Kansas, Oklahoma, and Montana, even though she was jailed more than one hundred times.

Women began to find strength in groups. One woman wrote in 1898 that if women gathered for any reason other than "the making of garments, or the collection of funds for a church," they were considered troublemakers.[2] Women continued to form organizations anyway, with champions like Caroline Severance leading the way. She insisted that women band together to gain respect and to improve society in general. In 1878, under her guidance, the first woman's club of Los Angeles was founded.

## The New American Woman

In most famous stories of the West, men stand at center stage, basking in the glory of triumph, while women are cast in the shadows. Contrary to these portrayals, however, women were not subservient helpmates. They were not passive and helpless. They did their share to make life bearable in extreme conditions, and they often took control.

Women helped bring to the West a sense of morality and respect by insisting on the construction and support of schools, libraries, and churches. Above all, women showed their true spirit in the daily tasks of frontier living. Traditional roles were as important as any others, and women stood tall in the face of such responsibilities. They chose to be productive, they chose to work, and they were determined to settle the West and make life worth living. Their resilience helped shape modern America.

# ⇥❦ NOTES BY CHAPTER ❦⇤

## Chapter 1
1. Dorothy Gray, *Women of the West* (Millbrae, Calif.: Les Femmes, 1976), p. 111.
2. Ibid. p. 112.
3. Ibid.

## Chapter 2
1. Dorothy Gray, *Women of the West* (Millbrae, Calif.: Les Femmes, 1976), p. 97.

## Chapter 3
1. Joan Swallow Reiter, *The Women* (New York: Time-Life Books, 1978), p. 24.
2. Dorothy Gray, *Women of the West* (Millbrae, Calif.: Les Femmes, 1976), p. 43.

## Chapter 4
1. Dorothy Gray, *Women of the West* (Millbrae, Calif.: Les Femmes, 1976), p. 115.
2. Joan Swallow Reiter, *The Women* (New York: Time-Life Books, 1978), p. 158.
3. Dorothy Gray, *Women of the West* (Millbrae, Calif.: Les Femmes, 1976), p. 46.
4. Joan Swallow Reiter, *The Women* (New York: Time-Life Books, 1978), p. 167

## Chapter 5
1. Grace Ernestine Ray, *Wily Women of the West* (San Antonio, Tex.: The Naylor Company, 1972), p. 9.
2 Ibid. p. 25.

## Chapter 6
1. Reader's Digest, *Story of the Great American West* (Pleasantville, N.Y.: The Reader's Digest Association, Inc., 1977).
2. Joan Swallow Reiter, *The Women* (New York: Time-Life Books, 1978), p. 104.

# ➤➤ GLOSSARY ➤➤

**annex**—To take over a territory, and claim ownership. In 1845, the United States annexed the Republic of Texas and made it a state.

**bankrupt**—To be unable to pay off debts. When a person or a business does not have enough money to pay off its debts, it declares bankruptcy.

**boomtown**—In the Wild West, a town that sprang up near an important mining stake, rail center, or cattle center. These towns often folded up as quickly as they started.

**cede**—To give power over a territory to another nation or government. This is usually done when the two nations sign a treaty. After the Mexican War (1846–1848), the United States and Mexico signed the Treaty of Guadalupe Hidalgo. The United States paid Mexico $15 million for California and the New Mexico territory.

**conquistadors**—The Spanish soldiers who first explored and conquered the Americas.

**emigrants**—People who leave their country or their home, and travel to another place to live.

**Franciscans**—A Roman Catholic group, or order, of priests and brothers. They travel the world bringing their religious beliefs to others.

**Mexican War**—A war fought between Mexico and the United States from 1846 to 1848, over territories in what is now the southwestern United States.

**missions**—Settlements founded by Spanish Franciscans in the New World. The Franciscans taught the Native Americans about Christianity and the European way of life.

**polygamy**—A custom of some peoples that allows a man to have more than one wife.

**pueblo**—A mud-brick or stone house built by Native Americans in the southwestern United States.

**rustlers**—Thieves who steal cattle or horses.

**sheriff**—In the Wild West, the chief law officer of a county.

**six-shooter**—A revolver with chambers for six bullets.

**Stetson**—A felt hat worn in the West.

**suffrage**—The right to vote.

**tipis**—A cone-shaped dwelling or shelter made of a wooden frame covered by buffalo skins. These were used by Native Americans of the Great Plains.

**wickiups**—A hut built by nomadic Native Americans of the western and southwestern United States. A rough frame in the shape of an oval was covered over with grass or reeds.

# ➤❦ FURTHER READING ❧◄

DeGraf, Anna. *Pioneering on the Yukon*. Hamden, Conn.: Shoe String Press, 1992.

Erickson, Paul. *Daily Life in a Covered Wagon*. Washington, D.C.: The Preservation Press, 1994.

Ferris, Jeri. *Native American Doctor: The Story of Susan LaFleshe Picotte*. Minneapolis: Carolrhoda Books, Inc., 1991.

Green, Carl R. and William R. Sanford. *Belle Starr*. Springfield, N.J.: Enslow Publishers, Inc., 1992.

Gurasich, Marjorie. *Letters to Oma, A Young German Girl's Account of Her First Year in Texas, 1847*. Fort Worth: Texas Christian University Press, 1989.

Miller, Robert H. *The Story of Stagecoach Mary Fields*. Morristown, N.J.: Silver, Burdett & Ginn, 1994.

Rawls, Jim. *Dame Shirley & the Gold Rush*. Madison, N.J.: Raintree Steck-Vaughn Publishers, 1992.

Stein, R. Conrad. *The Oregon Trail*. Chicago: Children's Press, 1994.

Wilder, Laura Ingalls. *Little House Books, 9 vol*. New York: HarperCollins Childrens Books , 1971.

# ⇥◉ INDEX ◐⇤